I0830588

BREAKING THE CYCLE:

HEALING WOUNDS, RESTORING HOPE — YOUR PATH TO BREAKING FREE FROM GENERATIONAL TRAUMA

BY SOPHIA EVERLY

All rights reserve. No part of this publication may be reproduced, distributed, or transmitted in any form or by any means, including photocopying, recording, or other prior written permission of the publisher, except in the case of brief quotations embodied in critical reviews and certain other noncommercial uses permitted by copyright law.

Table of Contents

Introduction: Understanding Generational Trauma

Imagine living a life where the wounds of the past seem to constantly echo in your present, affecting your relationships, your mental health, and even your sense of self-worth. These echoes aren't just your own—they've been handed down through generations, a legacy of pain that no one asked for. This is generational trauma, a hidden burden carried by countless families, and one that can feel impossible to shake.

But it doesn't have to be this way.

Breaking the Cycle: Healing Wounds, Restoring Hope is a guide to understanding and overcoming generational trauma—a process that starts with awareness and ends with freedom. By breaking the cycle, we are not only healing ourselves but also ensuring that future generations don't have to carry the same weight.

What is Generational Trauma?

Generational trauma is the transmission of emotional, psychological, and even physical pain from one generation to the next. It's the unresolved hurt, fear, and anger that festers in families, passed down like heirlooms, but much harder to confront. This trauma often remains unspoken, hidden in family secrets, unexplained behaviors, and patterns of dysfunction. It can manifest in many forms: anxiety, depression, addiction, abusive relationships, and more.

At its core, generational trauma isn't about a single event—it's about the accumulation of unresolved pain. It might stem from events like war, abuse, neglect, systemic oppression, or addiction. But more than the events themselves, it's the failure to address and heal from these wounds that keeps the cycle going.

How Trauma is Passed Down Through Generations

Trauma is passed down in many ways, from learned behaviors and coping mechanisms to deep-seated emotional responses and even genetic changes. Children absorb the emotional states of their caregivers, often inheriting fears and anxieties that don't seem to make sense in their own lives. Family dynamics play a significant role in this transmission, with unhealthy patterns like emotional suppression, avoidance, or aggression becoming normalized.

Recent research even suggests that trauma can be passed down biologically. Studies have shown that significant stress can alter how genes are expressed, meaning that the effects of trauma can be encoded in DNA and passed from one generation to the next. This revelation underscores how deeply embedded generational trauma can be and how important it is to break the cycle.

The Impact of Unhealed Trauma on Individuals and Families

The impact of unhealed trauma is profound. For individuals, it can manifest as chronic anxiety, depression, or a deep-seated feeling of inadequacy. Relationships suffer as unaddressed trauma distorts how we perceive and interact with others. Parents, often unconsciously, pass their unresolved issues to their children, perpetuating the cycle. Family bonds, meant to provide love and support, become tangled in pain and dysfunction.

At the family level, unresolved trauma can cause a breakdown in communication, trust, and empathy. Cycles of abuse, neglect, or emotional unavailability continue because no one knows how to stop them. But the good news is that healing is possible—and it starts with awareness.

Chapter 1: Identifying the Patterns

Healing begins with recognition. You cannot change what you cannot see, and this is particularly true for generational trauma. Often, the patterns of trauma are so ingrained in our family systems that they feel normal. But by learning to identify these patterns, you can begin the process of breaking free.

Recognizing Trauma in Your Family History

It starts with asking questions—sometimes uncomfortable ones. Take a look at your family history. Are there patterns of addiction, abuse, mental illness, or emotional neglect? Have certain traumas, like losing a parent early, financial

10

hardship, or other significant stressors, affected multiple generations?

Uncovering these patterns may require honest conversations with family members, or it may involve piecing together the puzzle from what little you know. It's important to remember that not all families talk openly about their struggles. Silence itself can be a symptom of generational trauma.

Signs and Symptoms of Generational Trauma

Generational trauma doesn't always show up in obvious ways. It can manifest as a pervasive sense of fear or anxiety, even when there's no immediate threat. You might notice patterns of self-sabotage, difficulty maintaining healthy relationships, or an inability to trust others.

11

Emotionally, you might find yourself reacting to situations in ways that seem disproportionate to the circumstances. Physical symptoms—such as chronic pain, fatigue, or gastrointestinal issues—can also be linked to unresolved trauma.

Personal Stories and Examples of Trauma Passed Down

Throughout this book, you will encounter stories of people who have faced generational trauma head-on. Their stories illustrate the many ways trauma can impact individuals and families—and the hope that exists in healing. These examples will help you see that you are not alone and that healing is possible.

SOPHIA EVERLY

Chapter 2: The Psychology Behind Trauma Transmission

The concept of generational trauma is rooted in psychology and science. Understanding how trauma is transmitted across generations is crucial to breaking the cycle.

The Science of How Trauma is Embedded in DNA and Behaviors

Epigenetics, the study of how behavior and environment can cause changes that affect the way genes work, has shed light on the biological transmission of trauma. Trauma experienced by one generation can lead to changes in the DNA that regulate stress responses, which can then be passed to subsequent generations. This means that

14

the effects of trauma aren't just psychological—they're physical as well.

The Role of Family Dynamics, Culture, and Societal Influences

Family dynamics—such as how conflict is handled, how emotions are expressed (or suppressed), and how members relate to one another—play a critical role in trauma transmission. Culturally, trauma can also be reinforced by societal norms that value stoicism or discourage vulnerability.

Psychological Defense Mechanisms that Keep Trauma Alive

Defense mechanisms such as denial, avoidance, or projection serve to protect individuals from the pain of trauma. While these mechanisms can offer short-term relief, they also keep trauma

15

unresolved, allowing it to pass from generation to generation. Recognizing and dismantling these defenses is a critical step in breaking the cycle.

Chapter 3: The Emotional Toll of Carrying Generational Trauma

Carrying the weight of generational trauma can take a severe emotional toll, even if you're not fully aware of its origins.

Emotional and Mental Health Effects (Anxiety, Depression, PTSD, etc.)

Generational trauma often shows up as anxiety, depression, or post-traumatic stress disorder (PTSD). You might struggle with feelings of worthlessness or find it difficult to trust others.

16

These emotions can feel overwhelming, but they are often the result of trauma you didn't cause—and don't have to carry forever.

How Trauma Manifests in Relationships and Parenting

Trauma often affects how we relate to others. You might find yourself repeating the same patterns in your relationships, perhaps unconsciously seeking out partners who reinforce your unresolved pain. As a parent, you may unknowingly pass your trauma onto your children, creating a new cycle of pain.

What the Physical Toll Trauma Can Have on the Body

17

Trauma affects both the mind and the body. Chronic stress from unresolved trauma can lead to a host of physical issues, including high blood pressure, heart disease, and autoimmune disorders. Healing from trauma is about more than emotional well-being; it's about reclaiming your physical health too.

Chapter 4: Breaking the Cycle: Healing Begins with Awareness

Awareness is the first step in healing. Once you begin to recognize how trauma has impacted your life, you can start taking steps toward breaking the cycle.

Self-Awareness and Recognizing Trauma Triggers

Healing requires a deep sense of self-awareness. Start by identifying your trauma triggers—those situations or emotions that provoke strong, often disproportionate reactions. By becoming aware of your triggers, you can begin to understand the root causes of your emotional responses.

Reflecting on Personal and Family Histories

Taking the time to reflect on your personal and family history is crucial. What patterns have you noticed in your family's behavior? What trauma might have gone unspoken? This reflection can be painful, but it's an essential part of the healing process.

Understanding Your Emotions and Responses

Your emotions are valuable tools for understanding your trauma. By learning to listen to your emotions—rather than suppress them—you can begin to heal. Understanding why you respond to certain situations the way you do can help you make more conscious, healing choices moving forward.

Chapter 5: Healing Techniques for Breaking Free

Healing from generational trauma requires action. There are many therapeutic approaches and practices that can help you break free.

Therapeutic Approaches (Talk Therapy, EMDR, Family Systems Therapy)

Therapy is one of the most effective ways to heal from trauma. Talk therapy allows you to process painful experiences, while therapies like EMDR (Eye Movement Desensitization and Reprocessing) can help you reprocess traumatic memories. Family systems therapy can help families heal together, addressing the relational dynamics that perpetuate trauma.

21

Mindfulness, Meditation, and Somatic Healing Practices

Mindfulness and meditation can help you become more present and aware of your thoughts and emotions, allowing you to process trauma in a healthy way. Somatic healing practices, which focus on healing the body from the effects of trauma, are also highly effective.

Rewriting Your Family Narrative

Healing from generational trauma isn't just about healing yourself—it's about rewriting your family's narrative. By acknowledging the pain of the past and choosing a different path, you can break the cycle for future generations.

Chapter 6: Rebuilding Relationships After Trauma

Healing doesn't happen in isolation. Rebuilding relationships is a crucial part of breaking free from generational trauma.

Healing Family Relationships and Mending Wounds

Healing family relationships requires both patience and effort. Trauma often fractures bonds between family members, creating rifts that may seem too deep to heal. However, with time and open communication, it is possible to mend these wounds. Begin by acknowledging the pain that has been passed down through the generations. This

23

doesn't mean assigning blame, but rather recognizing the impact of unhealed trauma on everyone involved.

Open dialogue is key. Family therapy can provide a structured and safe space to explore these issues together. By bringing the trauma into the light, you create an opportunity for healing and reconciliation. It's not easy to confront painful truths, but honesty is necessary to rebuild trust and foster healthy connections.

Setting Boundaries and Protecting Your Peace

As you begin to heal, it's important to protect your emotional well-being by setting healthy boundaries. Family relationships can be complex, and not every family member may be ready or willing to address their own trauma. It's crucial to recognize that

24

healing is your journey, and you have the right to protect your peace along the way.

Boundaries are essential to maintaining emotional stability, especially if certain family dynamics trigger your trauma. You are allowed to step back from relationships that are toxic or harmful to your healing process. While boundaries can feel uncomfortable at first, they are an act of self-care, ensuring that you don't get pulled back into the cycle of trauma.

Empowering the Next Generation by Fostering Healthy Connections

Breaking the cycle of trauma isn't just about healing yourself; it's about empowering the next generation. By modeling healthy relationships, open communication, and emotional honesty, you

25

give your children—and future generations—the tools they need to thrive.

Teach them the importance of self-awareness, encourage emotional expression, and help them understand that it's okay to seek help when they're struggling. By fostering healthy connections, you're building a legacy of strength, resilience, and emotional well-being that can ripple through generations.

26

Chapter 7: Personal Growth and Transformation

Healing from generational trauma is not just about overcoming pain; it's about transforming that pain into personal growth. On the other side of trauma lies resilience, strength, and the opportunity for profound transformation.

Embracing Resilience and Self-Compassion

One of the most important aspects of healing is learning to embrace resilience. Trauma may have shaped you, but it doesn't define you. Your ability to face and overcome the challenges of generational trauma speaks to the deep reservoir of strength within you. Resilience is not the absence of struggle but the ability to rise despite it.

As you heal, practicing self-compassion is essential. Trauma often comes with feelings of guilt, shame, and self-blame. Recognize that you are not responsible for the trauma you inherited. Show yourself kindness and patience, understanding that healing is a journey that takes time. By treating yourself with compassion, you give yourself permission to grow and move forward.

Personal Growth Through Trauma Recovery

Recovery from trauma often leads to profound personal growth. As you peel back the layers of inherited pain, you uncover your authentic self. This journey of self-discovery can reveal new strengths,

28

insights, and perspectives that were previously hidden beneath the weight of trauma.

Personal growth may involve setting new goals, cultivating healthier habits, or developing deeper relationships. As you heal, you'll likely find that the things that once triggered or overwhelmed you no longer hold the same power. This growth is the reward for your hard work and dedication to breaking the cycle.

Finding Purpose After Healing

For many, healing from generational trauma leads to a newfound sense of purpose. Once you have broken the cycle of trauma, you may feel called to help others on their healing journeys. Whether it's through advocacy, support groups, or simply sharing your story, your healing can inspire and empower others.

29

Finding purpose after trauma also involves creating a life that reflects your values and desires. You have the power to shape your future and live in a way that aligns with your true self. Healing allows you to move from surviving to thriving, embracing life with a renewed sense of possibility.

Conclusion: Living Free from Generational Trauma

Healing from generational trauma is not a destination—it's a lifelong journey. As you move forward, you'll continue to discover new layers of healing, deeper self-awareness, and greater emotional freedom. While the process may be challenging, the rewards are immeasurable: healthier relationships, emotional peace, and the ability to live authentically.

Continuing the Healing Journey

Even after significant healing, the journey is ongoing. Life will present new challenges, and old wounds may resurface from time to time. But with the tools and self-awareness you've developed, you'll be better equipped to handle these challenges and continue growing.

Commit to your well-being by continuing the practices that have helped you heal—whether that's therapy, mindfulness, setting boundaries, or cultivating healthy relationships. Your healing journey is unique, and there's no timeline or endpoint. What matters is that you remain committed to living free from the cycles of trauma that once held you back.

Empowering Others to Break Their Cycles

One of the most powerful outcomes of your healing is the ability to empower others. By breaking the cycle of trauma in your own life, you've shown that it's possible to heal. Share your story, offer support, and encourage others to begin their own journeys. Healing is contagious, and by empowering others to break their cycles, you create a ripple effect of transformation.

Looking Forward: Building a Legacy of Strength and Healing

As you look to the future, envision the legacy you want to leave behind. You have the power to build a legacy of strength, healing, and resilience for the generations that follow. By confronting and healing from generational trauma, you are laying the foundation for a healthier, more empowered future—for yourself, your family, and your community.

Breaking the cycle of generational trauma is one of the most powerful things you can do, not only for yourself but for those who come after you. The journey may be difficult, but the rewards—a life of freedom, peace, and connection—are worth every step.

This book is your guide to healing from the past, breaking free from inherited pain, and creating a life that reflects your strength, resilience, and hope. Healing is possible, and by breaking the cycle of trauma, you're not only transforming your own life—you're transforming the future.

Key Takeaways

1. Understanding Generational Trauma: Trauma doesn't stop with one person; it is passed down through families, influencing emotional and behavioral patterns. This transmission often occurs subconsciously, affecting both the individual and future generations.

2. Identifying Family Trauma Patterns: By reflecting on family history, individuals can uncover recurring cycles of emotional pain, behavioral tendencies, or unhealthy relationships that have been handed down. Awareness of these patterns is key to breaking the cycle.

3. The Psychology Behind Trauma Transmission: Science reveals that trauma can alter gene expression (epigenetics) and be transmitted through family dynamics. Unresolved trauma can be woven into cultural and societal structures, shaping how individuals relate to each other and to the world.

4. Emotional and Physical Impact of Carrying Trauma: The emotional weight of inherited trauma can manifest in chronic anxiety, depression, PTSD, and strained relationships. Physically, it can lead to conditions such as fatigue, digestive issues, and other stress-related ailments.

5. Healing Starts with Awareness: Healing begins by acknowledging and understanding one's emotional triggers, family background, and internalized responses. This awareness helps individuals reclaim control over their

emotional health and break the generational chain.

6. Therapeutic Approaches and Healing Techniques: Effective healing techniques include talk therapy, EMDR, and somatic practices, all aimed at releasing stored trauma from both the mind and body. Rewriting the family narrative empowers individuals to shift from survival mode to thriving.

7. Rebuilding Relationships and Setting Boundaries: Healing from generational trauma involves repairing family relationships by setting boundaries, fostering forgiveness, and nurturing healthy, loving connections that prevent future harm.

37

8. Personal Growth Through Trauma Recovery: Breaking the trauma cycle leads to deeper personal growth, resilience, and a newfound sense of self-compassion. This growth allows individuals to find meaning and purpose after healing.

9. Creating a Legacy of Healing and Hope: Once freed from generational trauma, individuals can help others in their families break free as well. This empowers them to create a legacy of strength, emotional well-being, and healthier relationships for future generations.

10.   The Ongoing Journey: Healing from generational trauma is not a one-time event but a continuous process of self-awareness, growth, and emotional renewal. It involves committing to the journey of emotional freedom and empowering others to do the same.

SOPHIA EVERLY

9 798343 789737